Also by Adam Zagajewski

Tremor: Selected Poems (1985)
Solidarity, Solitude (Essays) (1990)

CANVAS

CANVAS

Adam Zagajewski

TRANSLATED

FROM THE POLISH

BY RENATA GORCZYNSKI

BENJAMIN IVRY

AND C. K. WILLIAMS

Farrar Straus Giroux / New York

Library of Congress catalog card number: 91-76883

*Grateful acknowledgment is made to the publications in which the
following poems appeared in these or earlier translations: "Anton
Bruckner," "Sails," and "Covenant" in* The New Yorker; *"The Bells"
and "In Strange Cities" in* The Times Literary Supplement; *"The
Blackened River," "Cruel," "A Fence. Chestnut Trees," "Password,"
"A Warm, Small Rain," and "Russia Comes into Poland" in* The
Paris Review; *"Lava" and "At Daybreak" in* Partisan Review;
"Vacation" in Denver Quarterly; *"Seventeen" and "Without Form"
in* Western Humanities Review; *"When Death Came," "September
Afternoon in the Abandoned Barracks," and "Alma Mater" in*
TriQuarterly; *"The Creation of the World," "Presence," "At
Midnight," and "R. Says" in* Antaeus; *"Incorporeal Ruler" in*
Threepenny Review; *and "Spider's Song," "On a Side Street,"
"Burgundy's Grasslands," "Electric Elegy," "Green Linnaeus,"
"Watching* Shoah *in a Hotel Room in America," "Autumn," "The
Bells," "From the Lives of Things," and "Canvas" in* The Manhattan
Review

"So Low" appeared in Polish in List—Oda do wielości, *Instytut
Literacki, Paris, 1983; "Incorporeal Ruler," "In the Branches, Wind,"
"On a Side Street," "Night," "Matches," "The Gothic," "Moths,"
"Seventeen," "Without Form," "Wind at Night," "Wild Cherries,"
and "Fruit" appeared in* Jechać do Lwowa, *Aneks, London, 1985;
and "Lullaby," "Lava," "R. Says," "That Day," "A Talk with
Friedrich Nietzsche," "Sails," "At Daybreak," "Spider's Song," "The
Creation of the World," "Morandi," "Historical Novel," "Covenant,"
"Presence," "Russia Comes into Poland," "Late Feast," "Anton
Bruckner," "Elegy for the Living," "Burgundy's Grasslands,"
"Electric Elegy," "September Afternoon in the Abandoned Barracks,"
"Password," "The Blackened River," "Vacation," "Watching* Shoah
*in a Hotel Room in America," "A Fence. Chestnut Trees," "At
Midnight," "Eliade," "To Myself, in an Album," "A Warm, Small
Rain," "Autumn," "The Bells," "The Sea Was Asleep," "The Close of
Summer," "Apes," "In Strange Cities," "Moses," "The Light of
Lamps," "Islands and Towers," "A History of Solitude," "From the
Lives of Things," "Cruel," "Stones," "Alma Mater," "When Death
Came," "Simone Weil Watches the Rhone Valley," and "Canvas"
appeared in* Płótno, Zeszyty Literackie, Paris, 1990

Contents

CANVAS

Lullaby

No sleep, not tonight. The window blazes.
Over the city, fireworks soar and explode.
No sleep: too much has gone on.
Rows of books stand vigil above you.
You'll brood on what's happened
and what hasn't. No sleep, not tonight.
Your inflamed eyelids will rebel,
your fiery eyes sting,
your heart swell with remembrance.
No sleep. The encyclopedias will open
and poets, dressed carefully,
bundled for winter, will stroll out one by one.
Memory will open, with a sudden hiss
like a parachute's. Memory will open,
you won't sleep,
rocked slowly through clouds,
an easy target in the firework's glow.
No sleep: so much has gone on,
so much been revealed.
You know each drop of blood
could compose its own scarlet *Iliad*,
each dawn author
a dark diary. No sleep,
under the thick blanket of roofs, attics,
and chimneys casting out handfuls of ash.
Pale nights row noiselessly into the sky,
their oars silk stockings delicately rustling.
You'll go out to the park, and tree limbs
will amiably thump your shoulder, making
sure, confirming your fidelity. No sleep.

You'll race through the uninhabited park,
a shadow facing more shadows.
You'll think of someone who's no more
and of someone else living so fully
that her life at its edges changes
to love. Light, more light
gathers in the room. No sleep, not tonight.

Anecdote of Rain

I was strolling under the tents of trees
and raindrops occasionally reached me
as though asking:
Is your desire to suffer,
to sob?

Soft air,
wet leaves;
—the scent was spring, the scent sorrow.

Lava

And what if Heraclitus and Parmenides
are both right
and two worlds exist side by side,
one serene, the other insane; one arrow
thoughtlessly hurtles, another, indulgent,
looks on; the selfsame wave moves and stands still.
Animals all at once come into the world
and leave it, birch leaves dance in the wind
as they fall apart in the cruel, rusty flame.
Lava kills and preserves, the heart beats
and is beaten; there was war, then there wasn't;
Jews died, Jews stay alive, cities are razed,
cities endure, love fades, the kiss everlasting,
the wings of the hawk must be brown,
you're still with me though we're no more,
ships sink, sand sings, clouds wander
like wedding veils in tatters.

All's lost. So much brilliance. The hills
gently descend with their long banners of woods.
Moss inches up the stone tower of a church,
its small mouth timidly praising the North.
At dusk, the savage lamp of the jasmine is glowing,
possessed by its own luminescence.
Before a dark canvas in a museum,
eyes narrow like a cat's. Everything's finished.
Riders gallop black horses, a tyrant composes
a sentence of death with grammatical errors.
Youth dissolves
in a day; girls' faces freeze

into medallions, despair turns to rapture
and the hard fruits of stars in the sky
ripen like grapes, and beauty endures, shaken, unperturbed,
and God is and God dies; night returns to us
in the evening, and the dawn is hoary with dew.

R. Says

Literary rats—says R.—that's us.
We meet on line at discount movies;
at dusk, when brocaded suns sink in green ponds,
we leave the libraries, fattened on Kafka.
Enlightened rats, in fatigues, or in the uniforms
of an army mustered by a literate despot;
the secret police of a poet who might be coming to power
at the edge of the city. Rats with stipends, confidential
grant applications, snide remarks; rats with slick hair
and meticulous whiskers.
Capitals, burning asphalt, philanthropic dowagers
all know us well, but not deserts, oceans, or jungles.
An atheist epoch's Benedictines, missionaries of easy despair,
we might be a link in an evolution
whose sense and address no one betrays.
We're compensated in small, worthless gold coin,
and with the moment of bliss when metaphor's flame
welds two free-floating objects, when a hawk lands,
or a tax inspector makes the sign of the cross.

Incorporeal Ruler

Who owns the earth, you
ask, astonished. By day it's conquered
by square-skulled men:
police. At nights
we reclaim our homeland.
Who owns the leaves of the plane tree,
who tightens clock springs?
So many errors, with an incorporeal
ruler governing a tangible reality;
so many intermediaries, foxlike faces,
sly smiles, deceitful death.

That Day

That day, infinity, as though in sheer fun,
took on the colors of honey and soot; the hoarse cries
of the factories' whistles labored to express it.
Knife grinders ambled through yards
and left wakes of sparks, like storms without homes.
A squad of soldiers marched back from the firing range,
students circled the university.
The perfume of apples rose from cellars.
A tram nosed down narrow streets.
Black spruce trees cast just as black shadows on lawns.
A cat slept on a bench, as soft as a dream.
Someone practiced scales,
someone else lay dying in a long room.
That day, infinity, as though in sheer fun,
assumed the form of a flock of sparrows,
and, changing shape, pirouetted over the grass.

In the Branches, Wind

In the branches, the wind; lost, half asleep,
great traveler, libertine, frenetic
gossiper, and trees, knowing nothing,
stuck in place, stiff, provincial.
In the branches, the wind, and music will come
of that intimacy. Alpine sailboats,
broken firs, masts dreaming.
Branches like longing:
catlike they move
towards an ending Mozart glimpsed
in parts of his Requiem.

A Talk with Friedrich Nietzsche

Most highly respected Professor Nietzsche,
sometimes I seem to see you
on a sanatorium terrace at dawn
with fog descending and song bursting
the throats of the birds.

Not tall, head like a bullet,
you compose a new book
and a strange energy hovers around you.
Your thoughts parade
like enormous armies.

You know now that Anne Frank died,
and her classmates and friends, boys, girls,
and friends of her friends, and cousins
and friends of her cousins.

What are words, I want to ask you, what
is clarity and why do words keep burning
a century later, though the earth
weighs so much?

Clearly nothing links enlightenment
and the dark pain of cruelty.
At least two kingdoms exist,
if not more.

But if there's no God and no force
welds elements in repulsion,

then what are words really, and from whence
does their inner light come?

And from whence does joy come, and where
does nothingness go? Where is forgiveness?
Why do the incidental dreams vanish at dawn
and the great ones keep growing?

Sails

There were evenings, as scarlet as Phoenician sails,
that soaked up the light and the air; I was suddenly nearly gasping
for breath, blinded by the slanted rays
of the somnolent sun. This is how epochs end, I thought,
how overloaded ships sink, how the eyelids
of old theaters droop, and what's left is dust, smoke,
sharp stones underfoot, and fear looking like
joy, and the end, which is tranquillity.

Soon enough, though, it turns out to be only another
dress rehearsal, one more frantic improvisation:
the extras go home, swallows fall asleep
in precarious nests, the provincial
moon timidly slips into place,
robbers steal wigs, a priest writes to his mother.

How patiently you prepare and enure us,
what time you lavish on us,
what a teacher of history you are, Earth!

At Daybreak

From the train window at daybreak,
I saw empty cities sleeping,
sprawled defenselessly on their backs
like great beasts.
Through the vast squares, only my thoughts
and a biting wind wandered;
linen flags fainted on towers,
birds started to wake in the trees,
and in the thick pelts of the parks
stray cats' eyes gleamed.
The shy light of morning, eternal
debutante, was reflected in shop windows.
Carousels, finally possessing themselves, spun
like prayer wheels on their invisible fulcrums;
gardens fumed like Warsaw's smoldering ruins.
The first van hadn't arrived yet
at the brown slaughterhouse wall.
Cities at daybreak are no one's,
and have no names.
And I, too, have no name,
dawn, the stars growing pale,
the train picking up speed.

Spider's Song

All the life that once was is where?
Bygone civilizations, sunsets,
peaceful hill towns, spires;
where are monks' chants, flame,
what's become of past generations,
so promising, exultant with hope?
Where are pogroms, fear, blood,
throngs, screams, hatred?
The weasels of blessed memory,
orioles, poplars: do they peacefully rest?

I saw in a wood
leaves scorched by frost.
Spiders swung on long threads
as though playing with grief, and they sang:
What was, endures in imagination.
What is, waits for destruction.

The Creation of the World

Mornings, curled asleep in our soft beds,
and in history, cruel, sluggish, dark rings
under its eyes, mint leaves on its so weary lids,
mornings, birds impatiently strut
on the sill and call us to action. Furious
doves who hid behind curtains shriek
in hollow Mozartean tones: It exists! It's being built,
in the meadow and forest and next to the pond
where the odor of dry willow hovers
and a lark bathes in a puddle.
Up, quick, the rooster's running,
leaned forward like a sprinter; dawn
blushes, owls depart without a goodbye,
the insurgent flag of the darkness is fading.
Again silence falls, the great performance
delays, again sleep, darkness, the void,
nothingness, lack of presence, its specific
slumbering pleasure. Now rain dictates
a long, tedious lecture and typewriters hidden
in garrets lazily clack
their humid spellings-out, slow, hesitant,
like a small nation's unconfident leader.
But now the rain falls silent, the gardens resume their chanting.
They sing from the depths of their brimming green hearts,
arbors and trees, the core of their leaves.
A blackbird appears in the void,
perfect, full of pride, as all living
creatures are proud of their endless warm
virtues. Dew scatters
on the grass, each hard drop

is a whole, closed in itself like a planet.
A grass snake is suddenly here, then a roe deer,
a reindeer, an ash, a black poplar. Evil contents itself
for the moment with its stinging trope of nettles.
Suddenly newer and newer fauna evolves,
and new countries, wars, short waves,
long waves, the ax, the gramophone record.
Trolleys ring their great school bell
for a recess. Clouds swim on their backs,
gazing calmly at the sun. At last you awake
(though God made man first, really woman is older).
There'll be storms, abrupt dusks under leaden,
too heavy clouds; there'll be hail, frozen tears,
long journeys in quiet trains,
but not every thunderbolt kills, not every death
means an ending, not every speech missing means silence.

Morandi

Even at night, the objects kept vigil,
even as he slept, with African dreams;
a porcelain jug, two watering cans,
empty green wine bottles, a knife.
Even as he slept, deeply, as only creators
can sleep, dead-tired,
the objects were laughing, revolution was near.

The nosy watering can with its beak
feverishly incited the others;
blood pulsed wildly in the cup,
which had never known the thirst of a mouth,
only eyes, gazes, vision.

By day, they grew humble, and even took pride:
the whole coarse existence of the world
found refuge in them,
abandoning for a time the blossoming cherry,
the sorrowful hearts of the dying.

Historical Novel

Beyond the city limits, plotters scheme.
Judas shouts, "Victory is ours!"
An old prince snores in the palace. Chimes.
Scents of flour. A baker's apprentice's giant yawn.

The poet reaches for his quill:
shall he be tender today, or incensed?
In the theater Othello forgets his lines;
maybe for once Desdemona survives.

An emeritus scientist bends to his brass microscope.
The Bishop contracts for a lifetime stipend.
A printer sets an obit for the next *Daily Blatt*.

A child is born with an ominous horoscope.
A maid tears a page from a datebook.
Demons sleep, and reason. So much for that.

Covenant

—for Ed Hirsch

A moment of quiet covenant
in the Egyptian museum
in Turin; people and things, crowded
display cases, a German tour group's
noisy children, the watchful mummies,
annealed in the long fire of their contemplation,
lips tight as generals'
before battle;
the pyramids' granites, the statuettes
that protected the soul
from death and damnation,
until they were stolen
to serve no one again;
nail scissors
three thousand years old,
and my heart, as patient as a stammering
boy, and boisterous Italian families
loving their lives and their Sunday.
In proximity, shy,
without enmity, we were as one
and as one were aware of each other.
Time slipped like a copper pin
from the hair of a Pharaoh's daughter.
Blandly, amicably,
we watched one another, the old and young
of one world, mute and imperfect,
implements of desire and forgetting,
devices of pain and of love.
Even the polished knives that once could end longing
lay calmly on shelves, regretting perhaps

21

the tremor, the night plunge
in a breast, deception, dishonor.
Out the window, on the ocher-walled houses,
the sun rapidly wrote January's
festive proclamations.

On a Side Street

On a side street
of no particular town, extending
like too long a sleeve and raveling
into other streets
of different towns, an old woman feeds
stray cats and sleepily banters
with them, her fingers
licked by pink tongues, infinitesimal orchids.

Presence

I was born in a city of wild cherries
and hard-seeded sunflowers (common wisdom
had it halfway from the West
to the East). Globes stained by verdigris
kept careless vigil.

Might only the absence of presence be perfect?
Presence, after all, infected with the original
sin of existence, is excessive, savage,
Oriental, superb, while beauty, like a fruit knife,
snips its bit of plentitude off.
Life accumulates through generations
as in a pond; it doesn't vanish
with its moment but turns
airy and dry. I think
of a half-conscious prayer, the chapped lips
of a boy at his first confession,
the wooden step creaking
under his knees.
At night, autumn arrives
for the harvest, yellow, ripe for flame.
There are, I know, not one
but at least four realities,
intersecting
like the Gospels.
I know I'm alone, but linked
firmly to you, painfully, gladly.
I know only the mysteries are immortal.

Russia Comes into Poland

—for Joseph Brodsky

Through meadow and hedgerow, village and forest,
cavalries on the march, infantries on the march,
horses and cannons, old soldiers, young soldiers, children,
wiry wolfhounds at full gallop, a blizzard of feathers,
sleds, Black Marias, carriages, taxis,
even the old cars called Moskwitch come roaring in,
and warships and rafts and pontoon bridges roar in,
and barges, steamships, canoes (some of which sink),
barrage balloons, missiles, bombers,
howitzer shells whistling arias from an opera,
the shriek of flagellants and the growl of commands,
songs slashing the air with notes made of steel,
yurts and tents break camp, ropes tighten,
banners of dyed linen tremble overhead.
Messengers, panting, die as they run,
cables rush out, candles burning with quick crimson flames,
colonels dozing in carriages faster than light,
popes piously murmuring blessings,
even the moon is along on that hard, iron march.
Tanks, sabers, ropes,
Katyusha shells whirring like comets,
fifes and drums exploding the air,
clubs crunching, the heaving decks of ferries
and of invasions sigh, sway, the sons of the steppes
on the march, Moslems, condemned prisoners, lovers
of Byron, gamblers, the whole progeny
of Asia with Suvorov in the lead
limps in with a train of fawning courtiers who dance;
the yellow Volga runs in, Siberian rivers chanting,
camels pensively plod, bringing

the sands of the desert and humid mirages,
the fold-eyed Kirghizes marching in step,
the black pupils of the God of the Urals,
and behind them schoolteachers and languages straggle,
and behind them old manor houses skate in like gliders,
and German doctors with dressings and plasters;
the wounded with their alabaster faces,
regiments and divisions, cavalries, infantries, on the march,
Russia comes into Poland,
tearing cobwebs, leaves, silk ribbons,
ligaments and frontiers,
breaking
treaties, bridges, alliances,
threads, ties, clotheslines with wet washing still waving,
gates, arteries, bandages and conjunctions,
future and hope;
Russia comes in, marching
into a hamlet on the Pilica,
into the deep Mazovia forests,
rending posters and parliaments,
trampling roads, footbridges, paths, streams.
Russia comes into the eighteenth century,
into October, September, laughter and tears,
into conscience, into the concentration
of the student, the calm silence of the warm bricks of a wall,
comes into the fragrance
of meadows, herbs, the tangled paths of the forest,
trampling
the pansy, the wild rose,
hoofprints in the moss, tractor and tank prints
in the soft moss,
it overturns
chimneys, tree trunks, palaces,
turns off lights, makes great bonfires

out in the formal garden,
stains the clear spring,
razes the library, church, town hall,
flooding its scarlet banners through the sky,
Russia comes into my life,
Russia comes into my thought,
Russia comes into my poetry.

Late Feast

Evening, the edge of the city, a whole day
of void, then all at once
the late feast: the Sanskrit of dusk that speaks
in a glowing tongue of joy.
High overhead flow cigarette firelets
no one is smoking.
Sheets of blazing secrets aflame;
what the serenely fading sky tells
can't be remembered or even described.
So what if Pharaoh's armies pursue you,
when eternity is woven
through the days of the week like moss
in the chinks of a cabin?

Anton Bruckner

—for Renata Gorczynski

Dawn, and the scent of clover rises from low meadows.
Baroque churches press into the earth.
Peasant carts rumble through fog, geese quietly lament.
Practicing elocution like a timid Demosthenes,
the Danube flows over flat stones.
Mice run races through tunnels of hay.
In dark farmyards, lamps waver,
fearful shadows skim walls.
Sparrows try to sound human.
The manes of the horses are tangled, in the barn yellow straw.
Breath streaming, purple hands numb.
The world's too corporeal, obvious, dense,
its mutations have no design;
mirrors tire, reflecting
the same to and fro. Even an echo stammers.
At the door of a whitewashed cottage, a boy stands,
homely, with a too thick neck.
He is pious and good, though unappealing to girls.
Heavy boots, a bundle on his back.
Raindrops in a quizzical key drip from the roof.
The well pulley squeals, chairs speak in small voices.
The line dividing the spheres, where is it? Where are the sentries?
What do the elements lead and oxygen have to do with each
    other,
the torpid stone walls and the music that breathlessly
soars, freeing itself from the burden
of oboe, tuba, and horn, yet bound perpetually
to them so that the drums of hide
run with the spears of violas
and float in the rhythms of somnolent dances,

and in that breathtaking race, not, ever, a flight,
the shimmering Danube will vanish, and the cathedral of Linz
with its two domes, and even majestic Vienna, the Emperor's
golden grain sown in its fertile gardens, will fall far behind,
an insignificant dot on a map.
Anton Bruckner leaves home.

Night

Because you're only dead,
I'm sure we'll meet again.
You'll still be nine,
as you were when I last
saw you in the mountains.
A late afternoon in August,
ripe, transparent,
the cherry tree's leaves unstirring,
the grasses mute.
Currants, already black, burst
on the tongue, their sweetness
holding the memory
of spring and summer, of storms,
and mornings, and the flight of a lark.
Running before us, laughing,
you could feel our tenderness
that followed you as lightly
as the breath of a sleeper.
You disappeared into the trees,
the shadows of firs. Evening approached,
and coolness, in the green shade of the firs.
We stood in the last rays of the sun,
we called calmly, "Where are you?"
We were so close to each other,
with only the whistle of sleepy birds
between us, and the vaults of the tangled branches.
Night slowly climbed
its corridors and tunnels.
Night passed through day.

Elegy for the Living

The joy of the moment turns suddenly
into a black hood with openings
only for eyes, mouth, tongue, grief. More grief.
The living see off their days
that flee
like negatives, exposed once
but never developed.

The living exist, so light-mindedly, so nonchalantly,
that the dead are abashed.
They smile sadly: Children,
we were like you, just the same.
Above us, robinias blossomed,
and in the robinias, nightingales sang.

Burgundy's Grasslands

Burgundy's grasslands scale the hills,
then lie still, inert as clothes
on a hanger. Despairing, we know nothing, nothing.
Minimalist memory, restricting itself
to what actually happened, is helpless
before Romanesque schemes that weren't built.
A surveyor-raven methodically measures a field.
Ash trees no one would accuse of being aesthetes
erect lush, leafy tents.
Larks race madly from one cloud
to another, like waiters on Sundays in crowded cafés.
We know nothing. Weeds sprout faster than our thoughts.

In a village church not far from Vézelay,
there's no one but a priest, no longer young,
who sings Mass,
so utterly alone that the tear which gathered
for three hundred years behind the eyelid of a cracked bell
is ready finally to fall.
Then stops. No, not yet,
not as long as the lonely keep singing.

Electric Elegy

—for Robert Hass

Farewell, German radio with your green eye
and your bulky box,
together almost composing
a body and soul. (Your lamps glowed
with a pink, salmony light, like Bergson's
deep self.)
        Through the thick fabric
of the speaker (my ear glued to you as
to the lattice of a confessional), Mussolini once whispered,
Hitler shouted, Stalin calmly explained,
Bierut hissed, Gomulka held endlessly forth.
But no one, radio, will accuse you of treason;
no, your only sin was obedience: absolute,
tender faithfulness to the megahertz;
whoever came was welcomed, whoever was sent
was received.
        Of course I know only
the songs of Schubert brought you the jade
of true joy. To Chopin's waltzes
your electric heart throbbed delicately
and firmly and the cloth over the speaker
pulsated like the breasts of amorous girls
in old novels.
        Not with the news, though,
especially not Radio Free Europe or the BBC.
Then your eye would grow nervous,
the green pupil widen and shrink
as though its atropine dose had been altered.
Mad seagulls lived inside you, and Macbeth.
At night, forlorn signals found shelter

in your rooms, sailors cried out for help,
the young comet cried, losing her head.
Your old age was announced by a cracked voice,
then rattles, coughing, and finally blindness
(your eye faded), and total silence.
Sleep peacefully, German radio,
dream Schumann and don't waken
when the next dictator-rooster crows.

September Afternoon in the Abandoned Barracks

The sun, the opulent sun of September,
the full sun of harvest and stubbled field,
stood still above me
and above the abandoned barracks.
Silence
bivouacked where once orders
were shouted;
silence, not
soldiers; in the infirmary
silence, not the groans
of the ill.
The overgrown grass in the yard
needs mowing.
Silence where blue-skulled
recruits sobbed.
In me, too, silence,
no longer despair.
A black rooster, a hot, black banner of blood,
runs down a path.
Autumn fades,
war dims.

Matches

Nothing's final, not even
deception. Matches sleep in a cloud
of brown dreams on their back.
True fire hasn't been born
yet, godparents
wait, trout swim
upstream. Back home, small world wars
flare, a table
frowns, a curtain's brow
obliquely touches the street. Evening
is sad as a Jew whose train
hasn't come, and the stationmaster
suspects. This makes more
sense, perhaps it's a prayer,
don't rush, though.
Sometimes diminishment swells
like dough for a Sunday bread.
If I'm only part
of this poem, why does it all stay silent?
Why should God give singing to thrushes,
and bolts of lightning
put gloves on their flames?

The Gothic

—for Ed Cohen

Who am I here in this cool cathedral and who
is speaking to me so obscurely?
Who am I, suddenly subject to a new atmospheric
pressure? Whose voices fill
this stone space? Voices of carpenters,
ashes of ash now? Voices
of vanished pilgrims
who still can't stay still?
Who am I, interred in this slim vault,
where is my name,
who's trying to snatch and hurl it away
like wind stealing a cap?

Small demons in bodies
borrowed from bestiaries peer down
like swimmers from diving boards
to the ocean of green earth
below them.
            The languid demons
of torture cells in provincial
cities, small
communists with stiff little hearts.
Oh, they too were created,
like leaves, lizards, and nettles:
they bud on the church,
leaned out, half wind, half
stone, the rain
flushing their throats
like political speeches—progress,
party, treason: their mutters flow

like rivers poured
through the funnel of the larynx.

Don't listen to this cascade of artifice,
go back to the nave, the heart
in its ribs of granite, the whirling,
pointed life of the Gothic arches
lazily combing time, enduring
in their forthright prayer
like theodocies in a meadow.
Go find the height again, and the dark,
where longing, pain, and joy live
and faith in the good God who does
and undoes, kindles
and extinguishes, light and desire,
and who writes with his quill of years
long reminiscences
on the loveliest faces;
who tempts Abraham, casts up the domes
of Rome and the Auschwitz barracks, sings
lullabies to mute rivers and dims
in the lightning: go back, back
where concentration looms like a lake
in the mountains, where the metal
of illuminations and prayers cools.

Lost, circling in the cathedral
as suddenly vast as a Babylonian square,
evening now, dark, you hear alien voices,
whispers, calls: swallows
whistle, someone wails
with the voice of a suffering older than Cain's.
Far off, shutters close to stay closed
forever, and yellowish earth falls

on an oak board like a drum.
Someone is laughing aloud; you're alone,
no orator and no guide, trekking
a forest, huge ferns just out of sight,
herbs, flowers—white morning glories—
exhaling; sometimes the dead will find
a kind word, the ash leaves will glimmer;
owls flit softly through the vines
and the trees open, just this much, to utter
one sound.

       I feel
your presence in the bright gloom,
a sheet of torn paper, healing, healing
again, no trace, no scar. I hear
languages, voices, sighs,
the hopeful laments of those who loved
and those who preferred hatred, those who betrayed
and those betrayed, all of them
voyage in the labyrinth, above them
the fire soaring, the pure fire
of salutation and presence.
I feel you, I listen
to your silence.

Password

Look, your life, too, is becoming
the oil in a lamp on whose surface
the weak blue flame of homeland wanders.
That land, like depression, will steal
your youth and turn it into a password,
will take your rapture and give grief;
that land, that clock that won't run,
black band on a sleeve,
that land where souls are in storage
and bodies are no one's because death
is paid in advance and will come,
too early, at dawn, with its forehead of an ape,
too early, the clouds of morning, too early,
a prayer, kiss, the helpless children
fallen too early, and instead of orchids
the ashes of mountain September, cold fog,
the consoling lie, booze, not hell.

Green Linnaeus

Stockholm: green Linnaeus in the trees,
the conductor of an orchestra that's grown beyond him,
grows still beyond him, infinitely, with all its roots,
leaves, and buds, so that he diminishes,
grows weaker, less consequential, more brittle,
coated with verdigris like frost,
and yet he endures, if not monarch then guardian
of the forest, king of memory, scribe.

The one who carves up and diffuses the great current of creation
is him, the bald one, swimmer in the Eden-river of the Bible,
who must perish and surrender though his white arm
flashes once again a last sign over the abyss.

Music is a cave, I'll take refuge there,
the grotto of wingèd Latin nomenclatures,
where owls mean wisdom and don't hunt
field mice; in the cave, in the crevice,
in the entry of an encyclopedia I stand,
immortal, wretched Linnaeus, each day a paler,
more brittle bronze.
A shadow in the shadow of the trees, I stand,
like someone who has never lived in the world.
Above, my great disciples thrust up,
above, the green sky towers.
Passerby, one word of live language, please!

The Blackened River

The blackened river ran through the park.
Farther on, the numb gardens
were hemmed in by thick braids of hedges.
Where starlings sang now, a branch
of Auschwitz had been built:
under
the grass the dressings
from the Russian infirmary were interred,
so the meadow
is swollen and rich.
Gliders guiltlessly hovered in the sky,
in rain as benign as a tear of joy.

Moths

Moths watched us through
the window. Seated at the table,
we were skewered by their lambent gazes,
harder than their shattering wings.

You'll always be outside,
past the pane. And we'll be here within,
more and more in. Moths watched us
through the window, in August.

Vacation

The dark hair of summer. Beech leaves as tense
as the strings on a child's violin.
Rain, disoriented in the interminable drains
of a village church, blubbers.
Rembrandt, young, still unafraid,
watches from a postcard.
The sea lashes the rock so furiously
that someone mutters: war's coming.
Yesterday's sun still cools in the bricks.
Two cyclists in stiff capes
are crossing the bridge.
A green lightning of chickadees
glistens in the garden. The asphalt steams humbly
as though a barber had left his shaving bowl on it.
You sigh with relief: it's only
the weary pilgrims come home,
bearing the sugared bread of forgetfulness, exaltation,
silence.

Watching Shoah *in a Hotel Room in America*

There are nights as soft as fur on a foal
but we prefer chess or card playing. Here,
some hotel guests sing "Happy Birthday"
as the one-eyed TV nonchalantly shuffles its images.
The trees of my childhood have crossed an ocean
to greet me coolly from the screen.
Polish peasants engage with a Jesuitical zest
in theological disputes: only the Jews are silent,
exhausted by their long dying.
The rivers of the voyages of my youth flow
cautiously over the distant, unfamiliar continent.
Hay wagons haul not hay, but hair,
their axles squeaking under the feathery weight.
We are innocent, the pines claim.
The SS officers are haggard and old,
doctors struggle to save them their hearts, lives, consciences.
It's late, the insinuations of drowsiness have me.
I'd sleep but my neighbors
choir "Happy Birthday" still louder:
louder than the dying Jews.
Huge trucks transport stars from the firmament,
gloomy trains go by in the rain.
I am innocent, Mozart repents;
only the aspen, as usual, trembles,
prepared to confess all its crimes.
The Czech Jews sing the national anthem: "Where is my
    home . . ."
There is no home, houses burn, the cold gas whistles within.
I grow more and more innocent, sleepy.
The TV reassures me: both of us

are beyond suspicion.
The birthday is noisier.
The shoes of Auschwitz, in pyramids
high as the sky, groan faintly:
Alas, we outlived mankind, now
let us sleep, sleep:
we have nowhere to go.

A Fence. Chestnut Trees

A fence. Chestnut trees. Bindweed. God.
A spiderweb, the hiding place
of first cause, and the thick grass:
between its blades shine the proofs of existence
like negatives drying.
The smell of braids and of wind
plaited in the mouth of the loved one.
Sour, the crushed stem
under the tongue.
Blackberries won't be
the apple of our discord.
Windflowers by the creek,
a ball gets away from the girl
and ripe, yellow hawthorns
sway softly.
Turn off the glaring sun,
listen to the tale of the seed of a poppy.
A fence. Chestnut trees. Bindweed. God.

At Midnight

We'd talked long into the night
in the kitchen; the oil lamp glowed softly,
and objects, heartened by its calm,
came forth from the dark to offer
their names: chair, table, pitcher.

At midnight you said, Come out,
and in the dark there we saw the sky of August
explode with its stars.
Eternal, unconfined, night's pale sheen
trembled above us.

The world noiselessly burned,
white fire enveloped it all, villages,
churches, haystacks scented with clover
and mint. Trees burned, and spires,
wind, flame, water and air.

Why is night so silent if volcanoes
keep their eyes open and if the past
stays present, threatening, lurking
in its lair like junipers or the moon?
Your lips are cool, and the dawn will be, too,
a cloth on a feverish brow.

Eliade

Romania, melancholy, long treks
on foot or by kayak (the Danube storm
sparing your life),
then India, Lisbon, London, finally
Paris—the rue Vaneau—and on to Chicago.
He wanted to be like Buddha, or like Socrates,
leading us up from history's dark cellars.
Divine spark, he begged: teach me to laugh!
Divine spark, sustain the weary Moldavian exiles,
set them dancing, let them forget
their razed homes, the floods and the graves.
Jews: no persecution,
bliss and rapture await you.
Save us, divine spark, from the tyrannic,
trivial modern Nero and Tiberius;
air, open the gates of enchantment.
The most common objects—clips,
hooks, combs—have tasted infinity.
Don't the diggers find them
gently asleep in dust or in clay
as though Old Masters had dreamed them?
Occupants of this century, you must know
that joy flames all around us,
and that loving spirits follow behind us,
hushed, their clear hearts pulsing
as lightly as chimes in Mozart's *Magic Flute*.
The historian of religions—Cioran
wrote this about him—can't pray.
Salvation's a wave, high, blind, striking

the sand shore, if there is one: ocean,
black cloud, moon, the ruler of heaven.
At his funeral in America, the Eastern European
demons he found so intriguing
laughed, inaudibly, in admiration.

To Myself, in an Album

The grayish cloud flows fast,
the petals of peonies unfold,
nothing links you to this earth,
nothing binds you to this sky.

Distant gardens loom in the heat,
a cat yawns on a porch,
you walk a street of lindens,
but you don't know which town's.

You can't remember in which country
gleam airy starlings,
evening's step gently approaches,
rosebuds play hide-and-seek.

You're only an image, a dream,
you're made up wholly of yearning;
when you vanish, so will clouds,
you'll be a memory in sepia.

You'll haunt rural rivers,
and the shadows of trees,
but finally you'll subside, drowning
in the earth, in the earth, in the earth.

A Warm, Small Rain

Night, an alien city, I roamed
a street with no name.
Stone steps submerged me deeper
in otherness and thick spring.

A warm, small rain: birds sang,
guardedly, tenderly, from afar.
Ship sirens in the port
wailed farewell to the known earth.

In tenement windows, actors appeared,
from your dreams and my dreams: I knew
I was en route to the future, that lost
epoch—a pilgrim trekking to Rome.

Autumn

Autumn is always too early.
The peonies are still blooming, bees
are still working out ideal states,
and the cold bayonets of autumn
suddenly glint in the fields and the wind
rages.

What is its origin? Why should it destroy
dreams, arbors, memories?
The alien enters the hushed woods,
anger advancing, insinuating plague;
wood smoke, the raucous howls
of Tatars.

Autumn rips away leaves, names,
fruit, it covers the borders and paths,
extinguishes lamps and tapers; young
autumn, lips purpled, embraces
mortal creatures, stealing
their existence.

Sap flows, sacrificed blood,
wine, oil, wild rivers,
yellow rivers swollen with corpses,
the curse flowing on: mud, lava, avalanche,
gush.

Breathless autumn, racing, blue
knives glinting in her glance.

She scythes names like herbs with her keen
sickle, merciless in her blaze
and her breath. Anonymous letter, terror,
Red Army.

The Bells

—*for C. K. Williams*

We'll take refuge in bells, in the swinging bells,
in the peal, the air, the heart of ringing.
We'll take refuge in bells and we'll float
over the earth in their heavy casings. Over the earth,
over fields, towards meadows, carried
by young ash trees, towards village churches
under the veil of haze in the morning and forests
stampeding like antelope herds; towards mills soundlessly turning
waterwheels by the stream. Over the earth, over meadows
and a single white daisy, over the bench on which love
carved its imperfect symbol, over a willow
obedient to the will of cool wind,
over the school where Latin words chat
in the evening; over the deep pond,
over the Tatras' green lake, over crying
and mourning, over binoculars shining
in sun, over calendars which filled themselves
with time and lie at the bottom of drawers
as peacefully as amphoras in oceans.
Over the border, over your attentive gaze,
over the pupil of somebody's eye, over a rusty cannon,
over the garden gate which no longer exists,
over clouds, over rain drinking dew,
over a snail unaware whose statue
it's climbing, over a gasping
express train, over a boy
knotting a tie before a school dance,
over the town park where a Swiss Army knife,
lost lifetimes ago, lies hidden still.

When the night comes, we'll take refuge
in bells, those airy carriages,
those bronze balloons.

The Sea Was Asleep

The sea was asleep, only occasionally
did a whirlpool's sharp braid
or a shimmer ripple
its infinity-infatuated back.
As dogs dream of running,
we were thinking, that softly.
We spoke little,
walked warily
on the wet sand, and animal sleep
enveloped us like the future.

The Close of Summer

The commuter train speeds through detachments
of suburbs like a dagger hungry only for the heart.
The voice of some dictator or other
comes closer to me through the speakers
and a squirrel leaping from branch to branch
moves farther away.
The close of summer, cedar cones heavy,
a nun in a coarse brown habit
smiling like someone who's accepted it all.
Dragonflies skim the oily sheen of a pond,
rowboats slide then go down in the setting sun's crimson;
the heat, like a customs officer, palpates
each thing in its skin.
A mailman dozes on a bench and letters leap
from his bag like swallows; ice cream melts on the grass,
moles pile up mounds honoring swarthy heroes
nameless forever. Dark trees
stand above us, green fire between them.
September approaches; war, death.

Apes

One day apes made their grab for power.
Gold seal-rings,
starched shirts,
aromatic Havanas,
feet squashed into patent leather.
Deeply involved in our other pursuits,
we didn't notice: someone read Aristotle,
someone else was wholly in love.
Rulers' speeches became somewhat more chaotic,
they even gibbered, but still, when
did we ever really listen? Music was better.
Wars: ever more savage; prisons:
stinking worse than before.
Apes, it seems, made their grab for power.

In Strange Cities

—for Zbigniew Herbert

In strange cities, there's an unexpected joy,
the cool pleasure of a new regard.
The yellowing façades of tenements
the sun scales like an agile spider
aren't mine. The town hall,
harbor, jail and courthouse
weren't built for me either.
The sea runs through the city, its salty tide
submerging porches and basements.
In the market, pyramids of apples
rise for the eternity of one afternoon.
Even the suffering's not really mine:
the local madman mutters
in an alien language, the misery
of a lonely girl in a café
is like a piece of canvas in a dingy museum.
The huge flags of the trees, though,
flutter as in places we know,
and the same lead is sewn in the hems
of winding-sheets, dreams, and the imagination,
homeless, and mad.

Seventeen

The adolescent Franz Schubert,
seventeen, composes music
to the wails of Faust's Gretchen, a girl his own age.
Meine Ruh' ist hin, mein Herz ist schwer.
Immediately that noted talent scout, Death,
fawning all over him, signs him up.
Sends invitations, one after another.
One. After. Another. Schubert asks
for indulgence, he doesn't want to arrive
empty-handed. But how ungracious to refuse.
Fourteen years later he gives
his first concert on the other side.
Why does charity kill, why does being strong blind?
Meine Ruh' ist hin, mein Herz ist schwer.

Without Form

If there was just this,
a tree on which a star sleeps,
the empty cathedral at Chartres
and an impatient guide
and women waiting for their train
and music cold as longing?
If there was just this,
governments hiring ministers
and ministers hiring police
and a tiny angel
kissing their waxen lips in bed,
and dissidents protesting
and protesters marching
with smiling children
and music cold as longing
and the force never sleeping?
If there was just this,
poets' death masks and the skeletons
of giants in high mountains
and books on organisms' orgasm
and well-dressed blacks who don't
see me, and Keats crying
and those who're absent and traces
as light as the arsenic
in Napoleon's hair, and immobile masks
on petrified faces; the closed museums
of dreams and the force not wanting
to sleep and the masonic symbols
Mozart hid even in his Requiem,
so cheating God: so much unexpressed,

and women, who have to live in our moment
without having asked to,
and countries, free once,
peeled now like apples,
and the weather, which changes, and I, myself, mature,
without form.

Moses

Rivers rustling, martins preparing for flight.
Reeds like silent chaperons in ponds.
Mouths of so many cities, eyes of so many houses.
Glance of mankind, where are you?
Perpetual wind. Perpetual clouds, thirsty
for impermanence, drink time
as from cups stained with lipstick.
Farewell, warm bricks; shutters, farewell.

Day draws to its end, locomotives drowse
beneath plumes of flowering robinia,
snakes sway down narrow paths,
the small sun falls into a reed raft like Moses,
elated owls cry somber passwords,
a first star whistles in the sky,
the covetous fingers of nettles grow quickly.
Where are you, gaze of exaltation?
Everything's boredom without you.

The Light of Lamps

—In memory of Constantin Jelenski

A dose of death occupied your body,
but it does everyone's:
I didn't realize
it would conquer so soon.
You laughed with the courage
of a fire-eater of eternity.
As a soldier in your youth, you'd defeated
the Third Reich reading books in a tank,
but you marched the Boulevard Saint-Germain
like Montgomery,
against a sunset so huge
it wouldn't fit down the rows of buildings.
We knew nothing of each other,
being friends.
Now some streets are scars,
to be detoured.
Our one summer in the South was scorching; forests were afire.
In a Métro station in the suburbs once,
the two of us, foreigners,
disappeared into the earth,
in cold rain, the gleam of neon
dissolving in dampness like gouache.
In the kitchen of your flat once,
on the rue de La Vrillière,
we watched a white cat
drink from the tap.
There'll be no other "once."
You live in the shade now.
Moths should learn to navigate darkness,
since they so quickly find light.

Wind at Night

The wind rose at night,
the young, short-tempered wind,
a bubbling wine, Eastern prince.
It spoke indistinctly, in the accents
of languages living and dead.
Babylon's curses whirled within it,
the bells of Byzantium pealed.
Beneath its imperious blow, trees
obediently bent,
the shutters shook on our flimsy cottage.
We heard those voices with half
our attention, and, understanding little,
turned again to sleep, and to love.

Wild Cherries

Wild cherries sprout on slim
stems, pits wrapped
in pink flesh. Here, sparrows can spend hours
confessing to a stern vicar's ear,
loudly betraying non-venial sins
perpetrated at dawn.
Here, roses bloom half wild, too;
their petals hide missives
from the lost at sea and the unrequited,
to whom no one dedicates poems; at their cores
nestle quiet drops of dew;
bitter almonds. Sunday morning
a mother irons white shirts.
The State is perfect, the weather fine.
When you leave, the door immediately
weighs heavier than denunciation.
Thirst can't be quenched.
Behind the soccer field, wild cherries
sprout on slim stems, tart
by day, sweet when asleep.

Islands and Towers

Islands and towers I visited in the dreams
of my friends scattered all over the world.
They stood in the phosphorescence of memory, patient,
framed by towns at the limits of empires,
dried arbors, barbed hawthorns,
wooden steps bowed by the scuffle of feet,
in schoolrooms, hospitals like scars, concrete apartments.

Ironically smiling, you stood erect,
as though posing for a provincial photographer,
sure that we always know more than the film
can convey, more than a lens scrawls in its polar frenzy,
more than what's left of us
in an image, intention, thought, deed.

Snatched out of the Greenwich meridian, or Cracow's cathedral
where the hours are announced by a bugle, on leave from Hegel's
    system,
you looked at me with the open gaze of portraits
in the Louvre: in the street, streams
of spring rain flowed, lightning flashed
on the panes, stores of poetry melted.

That each failure is different: what consolation.
That each task has its own name,
each drama unfolds in a different place,
with a different ending; silence, tears, fright,
joy, vision, success, a hymn; it ends in a church,
empty train, jail, lecture hall, mud.

A History of Solitude

Birdsong diminishes.
The moon sits for a photo.
The wet cheeks of streets gleam.
Wind brings the scent of ripe fields.
High overhead, a small plane cavorts like a dolphin.

From the Lives of Things

The perfect skin of things is stretched across them
as snugly as a circus tent.
Evening nears.
Welcome, darkness.
Farewell, daylight.
We're like eyelids, assert things,
we touch eyes, hair, darkness,
light, India, Europe.

Suddenly I find myself asking: "Things,
do you know suffering?
Were you ever hungry, down and out?
Have you cried? Do you know fear,
shame? Have you learned jealousy, envy,
small sins, not of commission,
but not cured by absolution either?
Have you loved, and died,
at night, wind opening the windows, absorbing
the cool heart? Have you tasted
age, time, bereavement?"
Silence.
On the wall, the needle of a barometer dances.

Cruel

—for Joseph Czapski

In the Parc de Saint-Cloud, birds sang.
Alone in that vast, narcissistic forest
that looks out on Paris,
I pondered your words:
The world is cruel; rapacious,
carnivorous, cruel.

I circled the Parc de Saint-Cloud, east to west,
west to east,
I strolled through the leafless
chestnuts, bowed to the dark, bowing cedars,
heard pinecones cracked
by sparrows and wrens.
No beast of prey in the park,
other than time, just then changing
from winter to spring, stripped,
an actor flinging his costume away,
in the cold wings backstage.

Cruel? I thought. Here is the killer,
abetted by police and by priests—
even you've indulged it,
the protagonist
of your paintings. But is there a choice?
A world milder and softer?
Trees more exquisite, cedars
with still darker needles, more sumptuous
feasts, moments of meditation
thrusting to the core of knowledge?
Is there a kinder time, gentler, eager

to give back those we've lost, to restore us
to ourselves, pure, young?

A rose sky; tight, narrow ribbons of cloud.

The brown walls of prisons, hospitals, courts,
wailing corridors with no end,
moments of contemplation riven, imperiled
by terror, anxiety, lies.

I circled the Parc de Saint-Cloud, faster, faster,
winter over, spring not yet.
In the park, barren, bereft of its king,
I kept saying it, "Cruel," my only witnesses
lizards and birds.
Then, through a dense mist the white sun boiled:
I was impaled by sharp barbs of bliss.

Stones

Now you live behind the black door,
address unknown.
Perhaps you're hiding in the folds of the night,
but night comes and goes,
oblivious as a migrating swallow.
Windows open and close,
trains ride leisurely through the hills,
apples fall to the grass, heather breathes,
all beings are busy with life
and life lords it over the leaves;
even the stones are immortal and full of themselves.
It's raining, the docile city
is swaddled in longing and fog.

Alma Mater

Your alma mater. Red rock in a sea
of blasphemously blooming chestnuts.
Throngs of students milling
like detachments fleeing a battle.

You sought knowledge as if wisdom cared
for academic red brick and Neo-Gothic.
Your teachers moved their lips
like actors in silent movies.

Past generations were there
in the steep amphitheaters, too—
insurgents from lost rebellions
seeking solace in education,
and consumptive adolescents,
still ill beyond cure
(they longed for forgiveness, for having too timidly
lived, with partial passions).

At the window, the heaving beech.
A different message hovered in its leaves,
a different whisper, different alma mater.

So Low

So low, so low, under the flat
cap of the afternoon, as though
the Day of Treason had come when
they congratulate Judas. Time dozes on the doormat
like a greyhound. The still life
of the streets still survives, but only thanks
to your eyelids' untiring labor.
You'd pay pure silver
for a silence in which later you'd yearn
for an endless reevoking of a scarred
record of Mozart's Quartets.
So low, nothing; nearly nothing.
Not to be believed. To the point of distrust,
even distaste. But there is, there will be,
some trace of hope, a slim trail of smoke
creeping upwards like a grapevine's tendrils.

When Death Came

I wasn't with you when death came.
The municipal hospital was your last home:
white room, cobwebs, chipped
paint, a jar of cherry preserves,
an old issue of a rotogravure, a tin fork
with a tine gone, two glasses.
In the next bed, a tailor with cancer.
You were so old the doctors thought
you'd hardly weigh
in the numbers of death.
So old that the children on your street
thought you another century,
an empire slouching on the broken sidewalk.
As death came, though, youth came:
you suddenly spoke the language of childhood,
the white screen between you and the living
was the wing of a glider.
The intravenous drip muttered, a pigeon
impatiently paced on the sill.
You were taking all of yourself
from that dreary place into your death:
the dandy of eighteen, the mature thirty-year-old,
the German teacher with no truck
for indolent students, the pensioner
with his long daily walk
that may at the end have measured
the distance from earth
to heaven.
You'd regenerated yourself

for your death.
In the hall, the muffled laughter
of nurses; at the window,
sparrows fighting for crumbs.

Simone Weil Watches the Rhône Valley

"I found her in front of the house, sitting on a stump, sunk in contemplation of the Rhône Valley . . ."
—*Gustave Thibon*

Suddenly she doesn't comprehend,
but only watches:
the Valley of the Rhône opens in the earth,
old villages appear above it,
broad scrawls of vineyards, thirsty wells.
The plane trees slowly reawaken,
roosters resume their stubborn march,
hawks mount the sky again,
and now she almost sees the light breath of larks,
mounds shouldered up by black moles,
farm roofs, walnut trees,
church towers curled like tobacco,
dark fields of ripe grain, scythes glittering,
baskets of grapes.
In the shade of the juniper death hovers,
war is near.
The broad Rhône's mercury oozes down the valley
with its barges and boats;
a moment of forgiveness,
an instant's bliss,
the olive tree of nothingness.

Fruit

—for Czeslaw Milosz

How unattainable life is, it only reveals
its features in memory,
in nonexistence. How unattainable
afternoons, ripe, tumultuous, leaves
bursting with sap; swollen fruit, the rustling
silks of women who pass on the other
side of the street, and the shouts of boys
leaving school. Unattainable. The simplest
apple inscrutable, round.
The crowns of trees shake in warm
currents of air. Unattainably distant mountains.
Intangible rainbows. Huge cliffs of clouds
flowing slowly through the sky. The sumptuous,
unattainable afternoon. My life,
swirling, unattainable, free.

Canvas

I stood in silence before a dark picture,
before a canvas that might have been
coat, shirt, flag,
but had turned instead into the world.

I stood in silence before the dark canvas,
charged with delight and revolt and I thought
of the arts of painting and living,
of so many blank, bitter days,

of moments of helplessness
and my chilly imagination
that's the tongue of a bell,
alive only when swaying,

striking what it loves,
loving what it strikes,
and it came to me that this canvas
could have become a winding-sheet, too.